MONSTERS DO MATH!

DRAGONS DIG FOR DATA!

BY THERESE M. SHEA

Gareth Stevens PUBLISHING

Please visit our website, www.garethstevens.com. For a free color catalog of all our high-quality books, call toll free 1-800-542-2595 or fax 1-877-542-2596.

Cataloging-in-Publication Data

Names: Shea, Therese M.
Title: Dragons dig for data! / Therese M. Shea.
Description: New York : Gareth Stevens Publishing, 2021. | Series: Monsters do math! | Includes glossary and index.
Identifiers: ISBN 9781538257234 (pbk.) | ISBN 9781538257258 (library bound) | ISBN 9781538257241 (6 pack)
Subjects: LCSH: Science--Methodology--Juvenile literature. | Research--Methodology--Juvenile literature. | Dragons--Juvenile literature.
Classification: LCC Q175.2 S54 2021 | DDC 507.2'1--dc23

First Edition

Published in 2021 by
Gareth Stevens Publishing
111 East 14th Street, Suite 349
New York, NY 10003

Designer: Sarah Liddell
Editor: Char Light
Illustrator: Bobby Griffiths

Photo credits: p. 4 IgorZh/Shutterstock.com; p. 7 New Africa/Shutterstock.com; p. 9 (background) Andrey_Kuzmin/Shutterstock.com; p. 9 (dragon graphic) Shyshell/Shutterstock.com; p. 11 Evannovostro/Shutterstock.com; p. 12 StevanZZ/Shutterstock.com; p. 15 (background) relax_gap/Shutterstock.com; p. 15 (apple graphic) KASUE/Shutterstock.com; p. 17 fire art/Shutterstock.com; p. 19 Vera Larina/Shutterstock.com; p. 20 Ales Liska/Shutterstock.com.

Printed in the United States of America

Some of the images in this book illustrate individuals who are models. The depictions do not imply actual situations or events.

CPSIA compliance information: Batch #CS20GS: For further information contact Gareth Stevens, New York, New York at 1-800-542-2595.

CONTENTS

Words in the glossary appear in **bold** type the first time they are used in the text.

THE DRAGON DESCENDS

Do you see that animal in the sky? It looks like a large bird, but it has scales instead of feathers. And it breathes fire! It's a dragon! It's descending, or coming down, to look for **treasure**. Dragons are very **greedy** about treasure.

This dragon collects treasure—and data! Data is another name for facts and numbers. In this book, you'll learn that a dragon's data is more fun than its treasure. Check your answers to the questions with the answer key on page 22.

DRAGONS DON'T REALLY EXIST, BUT THEY'RE FUN TO READ ABOUT!

DIGGING UP TREASURE

The dragon lands near you. You're worried it might hurt you. However, it starts to dig! Its sharp claws tear up the dirt easily. You hear a *clunk* when it finally hits something. The dragon has found a treasure chest. It turns it upside down and different kinds of shiny **jewels** fall out!

DIAMOND

HOW MANY DIAMONDS ARE THERE?

RUBY

HOW MANY RUBIES ARE THERE?

EMERALD

HOW MANY EMERALDS ARE THERE?

Organizing data is a useful math skill that could help this dragon keep track of its treasure. Using the picture on page 6, answer the questions above.

MONSTER FACTS!

IN SOME STORIES, DRAGONS HAVE SHARP TEETH, LONG CLAWS, AND A POWERFUL TAIL. THEY MAY HAVE HORNS, **SPIKES**, AND WINGS LIKE A BAT TOO.

NOT THE ONLY ONE

You call your best friend to tell her about the news. Dragons are real! It turns out there have been dragon sightings all over the world. The dragons are different colors too!

The picture graph above shows the number of dragon sightings and the dragons' colors. This kind of graph makes it easy to count the dragons and to compare amounts. Study the graph, and then answer these questions: How many blue dragons are there? Are there more red dragons or green dragons?

MONSTER FACTS!

IN TALES FROM THE **MIDDLE AGES**, A BRAVE KNIGHT OFTEN HAD TO KILL A DRAGON TO SAVE HIS KINGDOM.

COUNTING HIGHER

This dragon is ready to head home. It has all the jewels it has gathered on its journey in its four claws. It looks like it found too many to easily count! Bar graphs are helpful when amounts are too high to show with pictures.

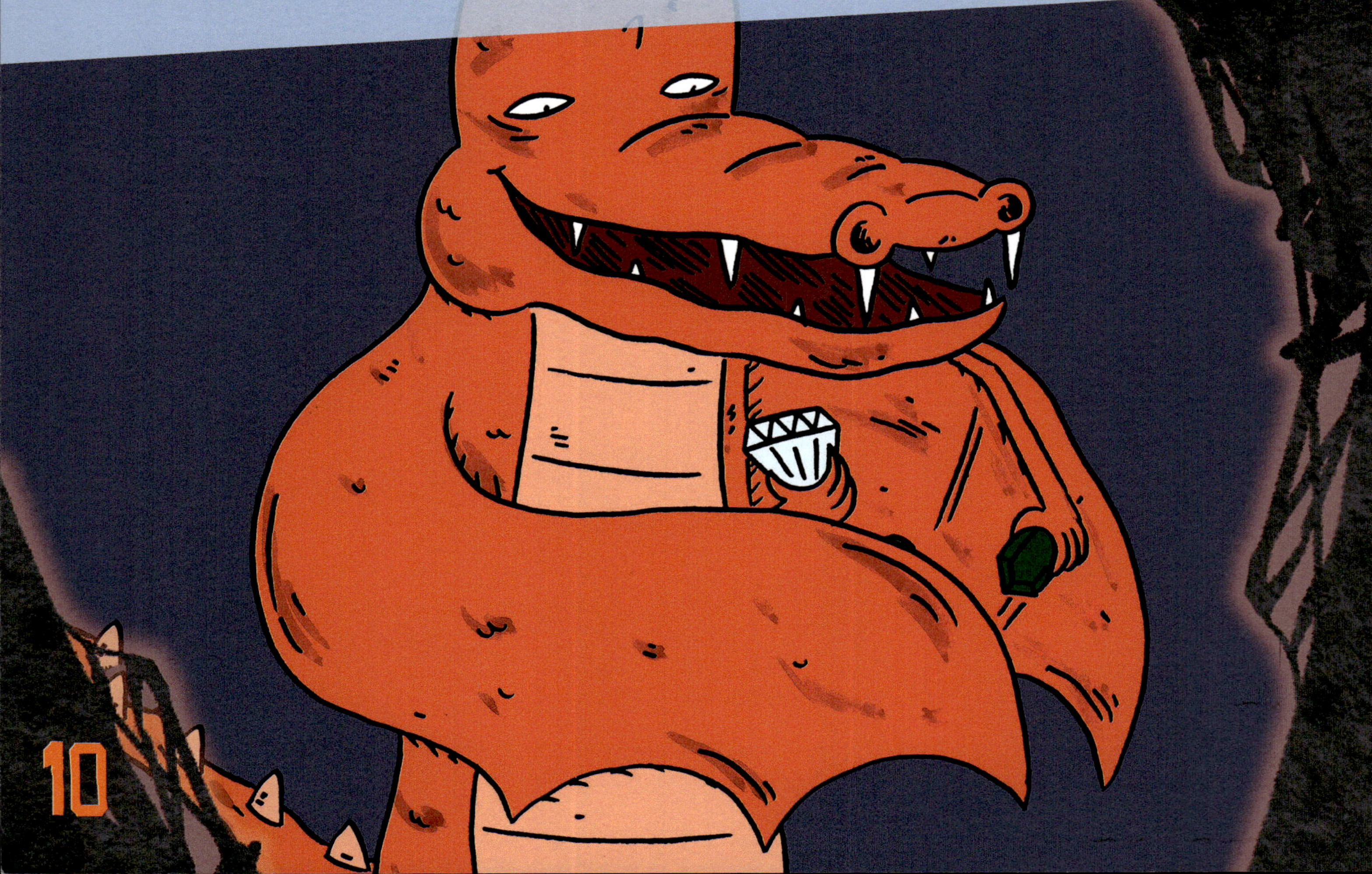

TREASURE TO GO!

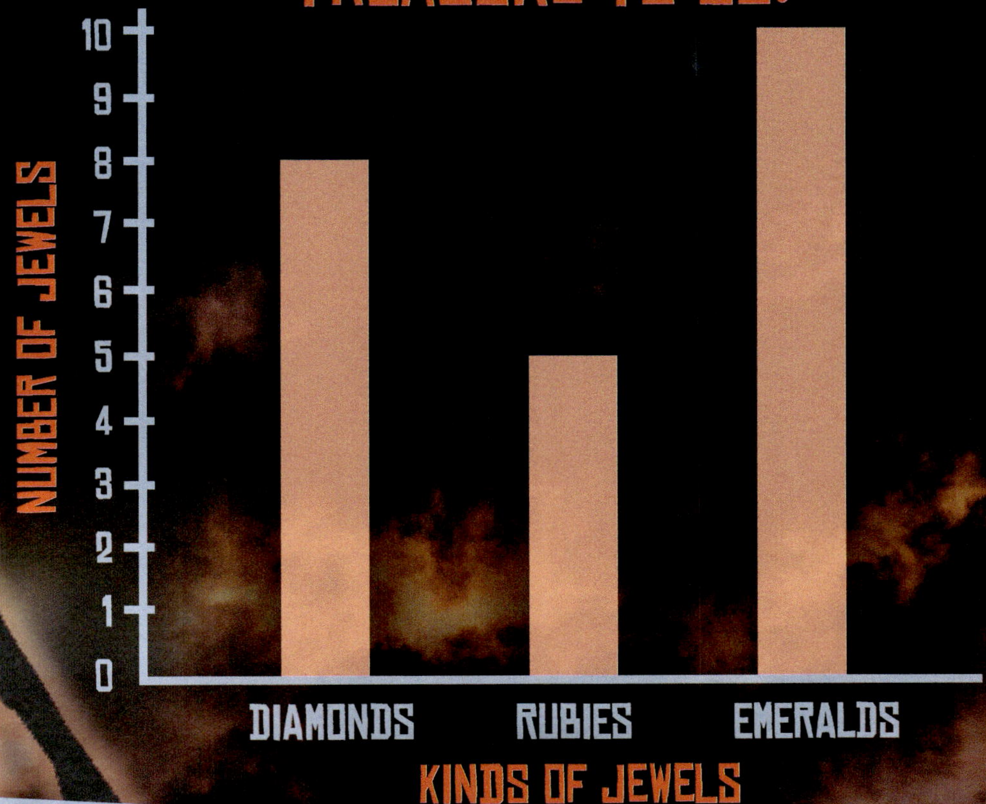

In this bar graph, each bar represents, or stands for, the amount of a kind of jewel. The top of each bar matches up with a number on the left. Use the graph to answer this question: How many more emeralds than rubies does the dragon have?

MONSTER FACTS!

IN TALES FROM CHINA, JAPAN, AND SOME OTHER EASTERN COUNTRIES, DRAGONS ARE GOOD LUCK! THESE DRAGONS ARE OFTEN SHOWN WITHOUT WINGS.

HOP ABOARD

The dragon points to its back. It's inviting you to take a ride! You fly over mountains, cities, rivers, and the ocean. You finally land on an island. Three more dragons come out to meet you. Let's get some data about these dragons! Gathering data can mean measuring things. You decide to measure all four dragons.

MONSTER FACTS!

SOME OLD MAPS OF THE WORLD FEATURE DRAWINGS OF DRAGONS!

LONG AGO, SAILORS WERE SCARED TO TRAVEL FAR FROM HOME. THEY THOUGHT DRAGONS AND OTHER TERRIBLE BEASTS LIVED IN PARTS OF THE WORLD THAT HADN'T BEEN **EXPLORED** YET!

You use your dragon measurements to make the graph above. Use the graph to answer the questions: Which dragon was the second longest? How long was it?

SNACK TIME!

The dragons circle you. They bump you with their noses and smell you. Are they getting hungry? You're getting nervous. A dragon leaves and comes back with a basket full of apples. They don't want to eat you. They want to eat apples!

DRAGONS EAT APPLES!

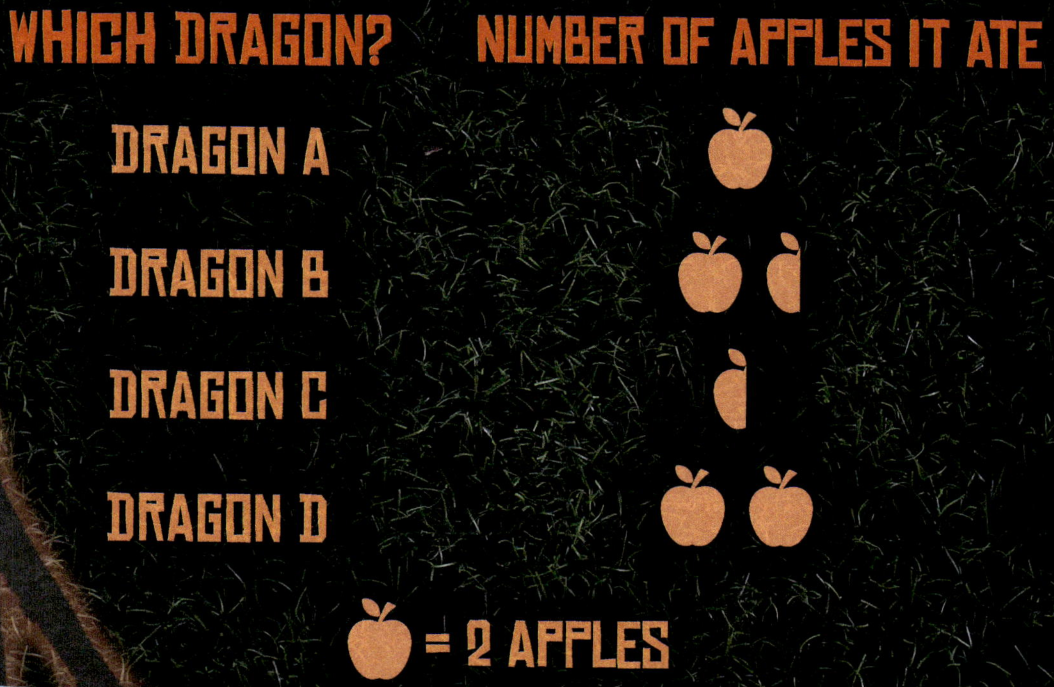

A pictograph is another way of showing data. The graph above shows the number of apples each dragon ate. Study it, and answer this question: How many apples did Dragon A and Dragon C eat? (Remember, each apple picture represents 2 apples.)

MONSTER FACTS!

PEOPLE LONG AGO MAY HAVE FOUND DINOSAUR **FOSSILS** AND BELIEVED THEY WERE FROM A CREATURE LIKE A DRAGON.

ONE, TWO, THREE . . . BLOW!

The dragons practice breathing fire! They ask you to measure their flames. You use a tool called a measuring tape to help. Luckily, you don't get burned!

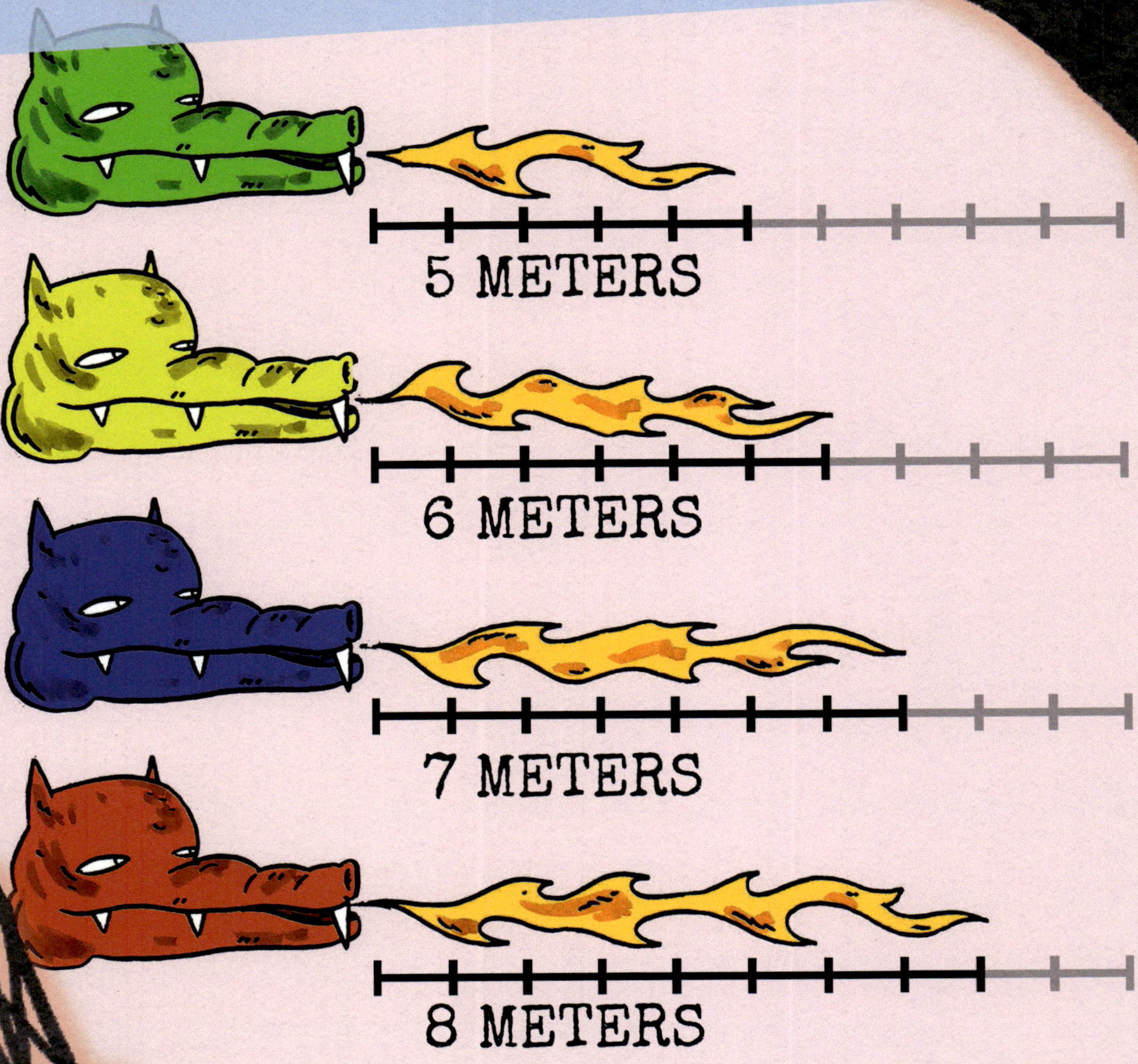

FLAMES OF FIRE

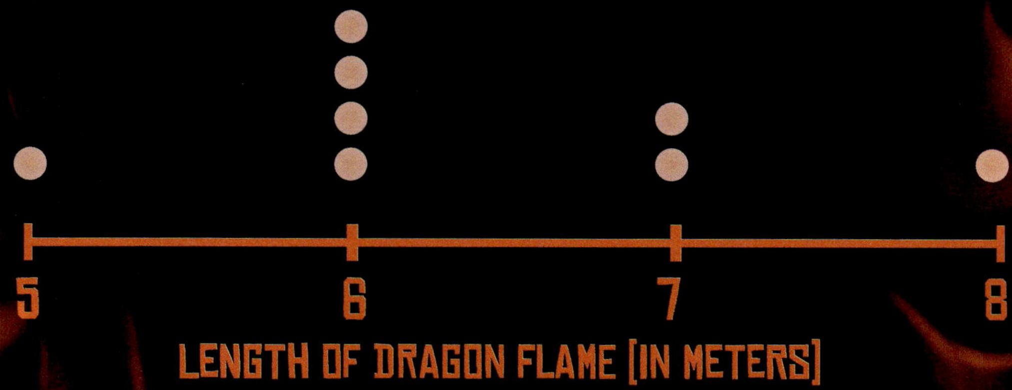

DID YOU KNOW DRAGONS USE THE **METRIC SYSTEM**?

After they're done, you make a graph called a line plot to show the results. A line plot shows data above a number line. Study the line plot above. Each dot equals 1 fire-breathing turn. Use the graph to answer this question: How many times did the dragons breathe fire 7 meters or more?

ENTER THE TREASURE CAVE

Dragons hide their great wealth in hard-to-find places. These dragons trust you. They invite you into their treasure cave. You can't believe your eyes. The cave is filled with jewels and gold. That means it's filled with data too!

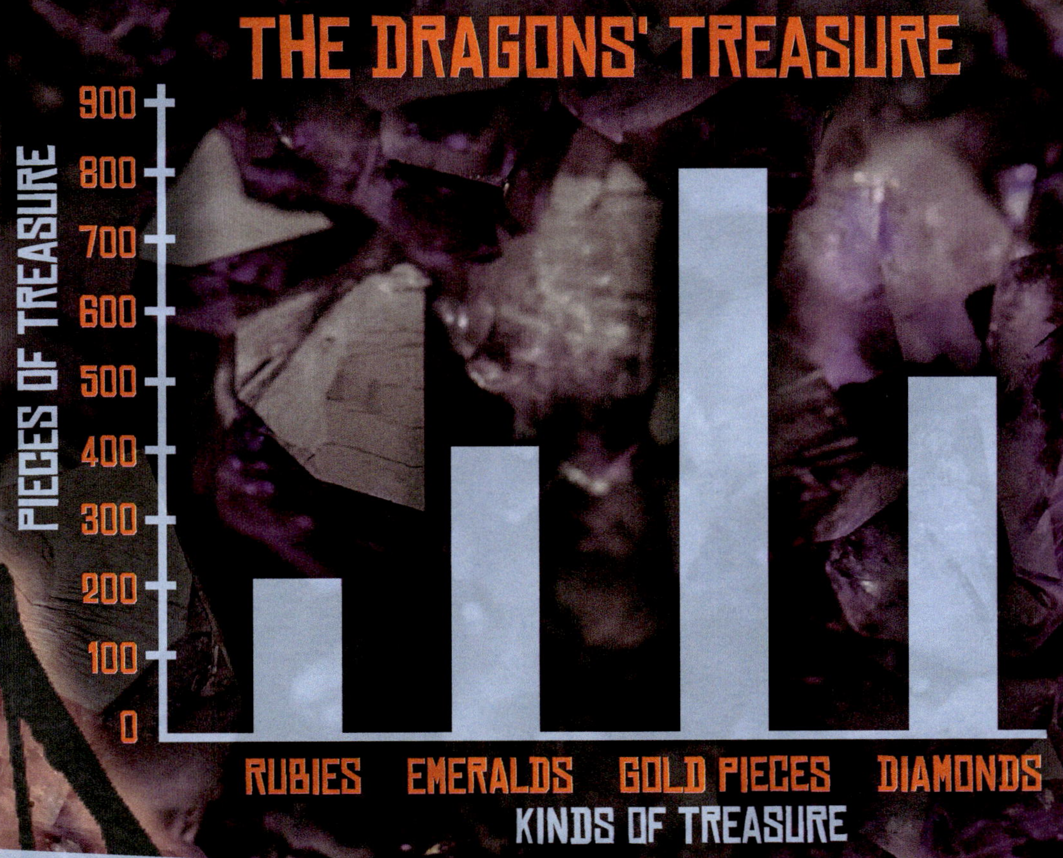

The dragons need your help counting and organizing the treasure. You draw a bar graph to help them. Use the bar graph above to answer these questions: How many gold pieces are there? How many more diamonds than emeralds are there?

MONSTER FACTS!

FAMOUS MOVIES WITH A DRAGON INCLUDE *MULAN*, *PETE'S DRAGON*, AND THE *HOW TO TRAIN YOUR DRAGON* MOVIES.

THE JOURNEY HOME

The dragons are thankful for your help. They give you a gold coin for your good work! Sadly, it's time to go home. You hold on tight to a dragon and enjoy the view on the journey home. You learned so much about dragons—and about what to do with data.

Now you know how to collect and organize measurements and amounts in helpful ways. You can also make different kinds of graphs with data. How else can you use these skills in your life?

THE NEXT TIME YOU DEAL WITH DATA, THINK OF THE DRAGONS THAT HELPED YOU FIGURE OUT HOW TO ORGANIZE AND STUDY IT!

GLOSSARY

explore: to search in order to find out new things

fossil: the marks or remains of plants and animals that formed over thousands or millions of years

greedy: having a strong wish for more goods than needed

jewel: a valuable stone that people often cut and polish

metric system: a set of measurements based on units, or amounts, such as the liter and meter

Middle Ages: a time in European history from about 500 to 1500

organize: to put together in an orderly way

spike: a sharp part of something

treasure: something of value that's often hidden or kept in a safe place

ANSWER KEY

p. 7: 5 diamonds; 4 rubies; 3 emeralds

p. 9: 5 blue dragons; more red dragons

p. 11: 5 more emeralds

p. 13: Dragon C (red); 20 feet

p. 15: 3 apples

p. 17: 3 times

p. 19: 800 gold pieces; 100 more diamonds

FOR MORE INFORMATION

BOOKS

Alberti, Theresa Jarosz. *Dragons*. New York, NY: AV2 by Weigl, 2020.

Flatt, Lizann. *Collecting Data*. New York, NY: Crabtree Publishing Company, 2017.

Heos, Bridget. *Making Graphs*. Mankato, MN. Riverstream Publishing, 2015.

WEBSITES

European Dragons
www.amnh.org/exhibitions/mythic-creatures/dragons/european-dragons
Discover what people have written about dragons in the past.

Mythology
www.ducksters.com/history/china/chinese_mythology.php
Read a bit about dragons and other myths of China.

Reading Picture Graphs
www.khanacademy.org/math/cc-third-grade-math/represent-and-interpret-data/imp-picture-graphs/a/create-pic-graphs.
Learn about reading and creating fun picture graphs here.

Publisher's note to educators and parents: Our editors have carefully reviewed these websites to ensure that they are suitable for students. Many websites change frequently, however, and we cannot guarantee that a site's future contents will continue to meet our high standards of quality and educational value. Be advised that students should be closely supervised whenever they access the internet.

INDEX